7/00-6 (12/99)

5-01	6	12-99
1/04	9	1/03
9/05	12-1	3/05
8/07	12-1	3/05
5-12	18-1	12-11-11

SEP 1995

THE ILLUSTRATED MOTORCYCLE LEGENDS

ROY BACON

CHARTWELL
BOOKS, INC.

Previous page: The Trident 900 of 1992.

Acknowledgements

The author and publishers wish to acknowledge their debt to all who loaned material and photographs for this book. Sources were the National Motor Museum at Beaulieu, Motor Cycle News courtesy of editor Rob Munro-Hall, EMAP whose archives hold the old Motor Cycle Weekly files, the Mick Woolett archive, Jim Davies, Ian Kennedy, John Cooper who took the photos of Ian's finely restored TR6 and T120, the new Triumph firm at Hinckley and the author's own files which include material from the Meriden Triumph. Thanks to all who helped.

Published by
CHARTWELL BOOKS. INC.
A division of **BOOK SALES, INC.**
110 Enterprise Avenue
Secaucus, New Jersey 07094

ISBN 0-7858-0005-0

Designed by Anthony Cohen

Printed and bound in China

Contents

EDWARDIAN BEGINNINGS

T riumph - a marque that was born in Edwardian times and flourishes today, as popular as ever. A dominant and most important British company, but one founded by two Germans. A firm which stuck to the conventional and avoided change in its early days, but whose innovation set the postwar trend of the motorcycle for a quarter of a century.

The firm was founded by Siegfried Bettmann in 1886, beginning with bicycles, as did many in the industry. He chose the company name to be acceptable in Britain and easy to translate to other European tongues, being joined in the late-Victorian period by Mauritz Schulte. Although they parted after a quarrel in 1919, their work in the Edwardian era did much to keep the British industry alive. While others indulged in fancy, Schulte concentrated on the production of simple, basic, reliable machines, built to a high quality standard so they soon won their 'Trusty' nickname.

Triumph were based in Coventry and built their first motorcycle in 1902. Typical of that time, it had an imported Minerva engine hung from the downtube of a heavy-duty roadster bicycle, driving the rear wheel directly by belt. Other machines followed using British engines, but this was just an interim stage.

The first Triumph motorcycle of 1902 showed the firm's bicycle origins and fitted a Belgian 2-hp Minerva engine.

By 1904 the engine was upright, still Belgian, but a 3-hp Fafnir. Direct belt drive and rigid forks made riding hard work.

In 1905 Triumph began to make their own 3-hp engine which was simple, basic and successful. The next year brought their famous rocking front fork which pivoted about the bottom crown against springs at the top. Not as good as other types, and a danger if the spring broke, it remained in use until the early-1920s.

During the Edwardian decade, Triumph concentrated on one basic model which they sought to improve for the buying public; better materials and processes to reduce wear and increase efficiency were their goal. Other firms were more radical and most fell by the wayside. The Triumph did enlarge to 3.5-hp, it did become available with the variable pulley, hub gears and hub clutch of the time, but the 1914 model still looked much as that of 1905. By then it was dated and had been joined by a Junior machine, this having a 225cc two-stroke engine, two-speed gearbox, belt final drive and the Triumph front fork.

Not that the firm shunned publicity. A Triumph won the 1908 TT and Ivan Hart-Davies used the make for his End-to-End rides from John O'Groats to Lands End, his last in 1911 covering the 886 miles in 29 hours 12 minutes despite pushing the last mile. The average was just over 30 mph.

By 1914 the marque was well established but then came the Great War and Triumph geared up to supply the services with some 30,000 machines. From 1915 they built the 550cc model H, this having a chain-driven, three-speed countershaft gearbox and clutch, although it retained the belt final drive. It was a form which served them well for years.

The Triumph Junior, having a 225cc two-stroke engine and two-speed gearbox, which was built from 1914 to 1925 and known as the 'Baby'.

Percy Butler seated on the Triumph he took to 16th place in the 1912 Senior TT, an event the marque had won in 1908.

World War 1 and 30,000 model H Triumphs served the forces, many in the mud of Flanders.

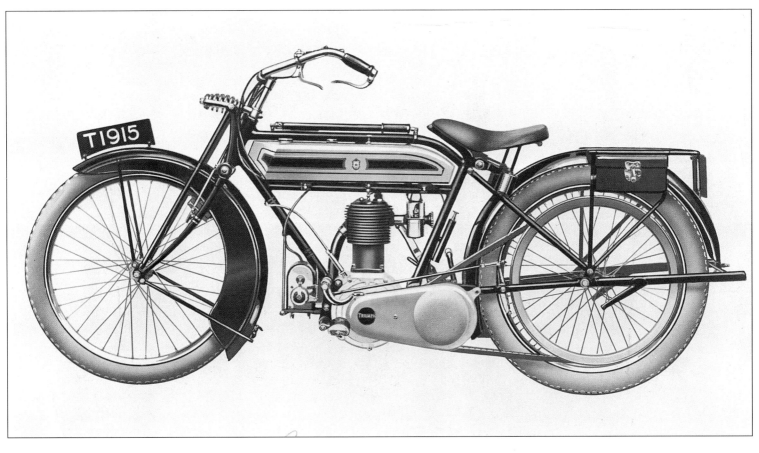

The famous 550cc model H of 1915, based on the older machine but enlarged and with gearbox and clutch.

Triumph testers in 1919 ready to give models H and Junior their brief run on the road before despatch to a public desperate for transport.

TWENTIES

After the conflict the firm picked up where it had left off, producing the models H and Junior, joined in 1920 by the all-chain-drive 550cc SD, a good move forward. The famous 499cc sports Ricardo model having a four-valve head came in for 1922 and, inevitably, the young bloods of the day christened it the 'Riccy'. It was based on machines raced in the 1921 TT, was second in the 1922 TT, broke records at Brooklands and remained a production model until 1927, albeit with limited development.

For 1923 the Junior stretched out to 249cc, but was dropped two years later. It was joined by the model LS, a neat 346cc of unit-construction, three speeds and gear primary drive, the magneto being driven from the gearbox. It had Druid front forks and a drum front brake, a much needed fitting also used by the Riccy.

As the mid-1920s approached trade went down and to combat this Triumph introduced the 493cc model P for 1925, this having a rock-bottom price to sell far below its rivals. The first batch was a massive 20,000 machines, the model sold well, and production rose to 1,000 machines per week. This despite some shortcomings concerning penny-pinching details.

To the firm's credit, the second batch had most of the faults eradicated and this pulled Triumph along for a year or two while variations on the basic theme were added for buyers having slightly deeper purses. An oddball appeared as the 274cc model W, this capacity being arrived at as offering as much engine as possible while keeping below a road tax weight limit.

All this kept the firm busy, especially as they had moved into car production in 1923, so that their eight-model range for 1927, plus the introduction of the Super Seven car for 1928, stretched them too far. The range shrank, but increased again for 1929 when all but one model were updated by the fitting of saddle tanks. This, and other changes, moved the style out of the vintage era and prepared for the depressed years ahead.

An early-postwar model H outfit, the alternative SD had all-chain drive by then, well worth the extra cost.

The Ricardo model of 1922 which had four overhead valves for its 499cc engine, but still kept the bicycle-type front brake.

Advertising stunt used to promote the
ultra-cheap model P and its slightly
upmarket brother, the model Q,
both having 493cc engines.

By 1924 this 550cc SD model was well
established in the range.

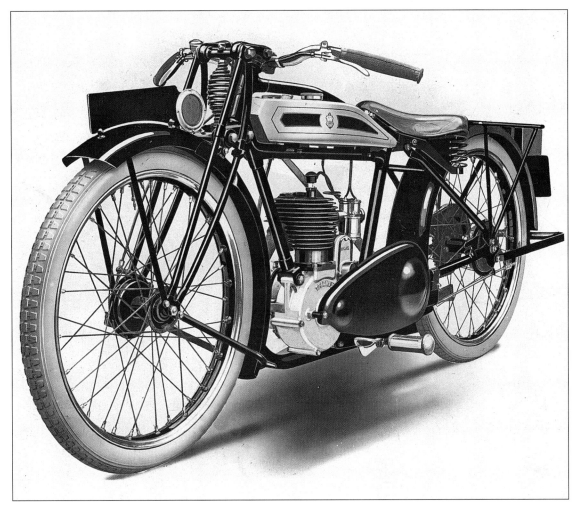

Above: This 346cc model LS appeared for 1924, having unit construction among its features, but was only built for four years.

Left: Aimed to give the maximum capacity within a tax weight limit, the model W of 1927 had the odd engine size of 274cc.

Below: By 1927 the Ricardo had been replaced by this model TT whose engine was based on experience gained racing at Brooklands.

THIRTIES – AND TIGERS

The range was further revised for 1930 and 1931, adding a small 175cc two-stroke, the model X or Junior, and then an ohv 250 to help in the desperate hunt for customers. The model X was technically original in having unit construction for its two-speed gearbox, the crankshaft itself carrying the two driving gears, but was only listed for three years.

Inclined engines were the fashion for 1931, while 1932 brought quiet models listed as Silent Scouts. To suit a reduced-tax class for small machines, there were 150cc two-stroke, and later ohv four-stroke models of the same size. These measures kept the firm alive until 1934 when a new range appeared, little of the past surviving.

The new models were designed by Val Page, who had moved over from Ariel, and his brilliance produced the simple reliable models the times and the market demanded. The engines came in 250, 350 and 500 capacities, had side or overhead valves, but were all basic four-stroke singles fitted into conventional cycle parts. They were worthy, if not glamorous.

With the singles there was a 647cc vertical twin aimed at the sidecar market. This also was well built and worthy, was offered with its own sidecar, won the prestigious Maudes Trophy (an indicator of overall excellence for a road model), but failed to sell well during its three-year life.

The 1934 range stabilised the motorcycle business, but the car side ran the firm into financial difficulties and it seemed that it would fail at the end of 1935. Fortunately, Jack Sangster, whose family had controlled Ariel from Victorian times, was able to move in and take over Triumph motorcycles which split from the cars.

Sangster appointed Edward Turner as General Manager, moving him from Ariel with a brief to revitalise the firm and in this he was successful, if ruthless. By all accounts, Turner was hard and demanding, but able to command great loyalty from

The sports model for 1930 was this 498cc, ohv, model CTT which retained the twin-port cylinder head and two exhaust systems despite the hard times

his staff, and with a unique ability to see what the public would buy.

His first move at Triumph was to add the Tiger 70, 80 and 90 models to the range; effectively the sports versions of existing 250, 350 and 500 ohv machines. Turner added highly polished cases, upswept exhausts, petrol tanks in chrome-plate and silver sheen, plus the evocative names with their suggestion of the model's speed. It was a brilliant move and fitted the times well for the depression years were passing and the public were looking for more colour and sparkle. The firm won the Maudes Trophy again in 1937, having added a 600cc side-valve model for sidecar work, and improved lines and finish for all models.

Left: Bottom end of the range for 1930 was this model X, or Junior, which had a two-stroke engine. A depression special.

Below: Fashion decreed that engines should be inclined for 1931, so Triumph duly obliged, this model being the 249cc W0.

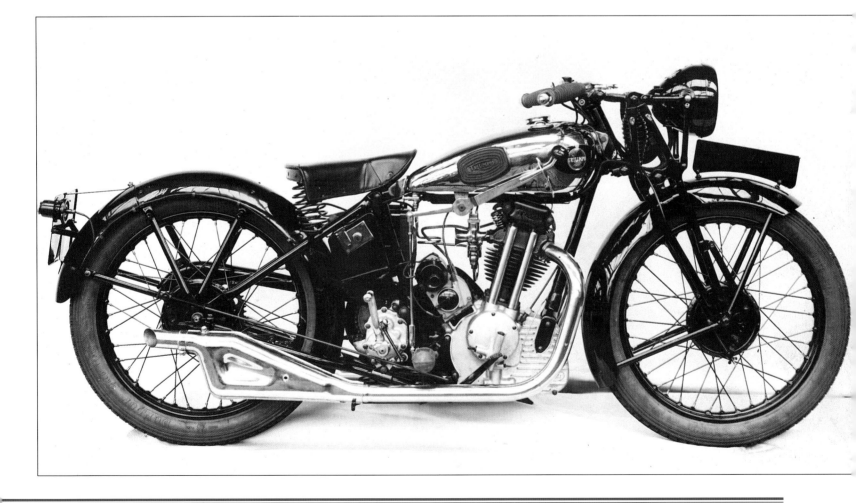

Another 1931 model, the 343cc NM which was only listed for two years.

The 1932 model CD of 493cc capacity, fitted with Bowden carburettor and carrying its engine oil in the forward part of the crankcase.

The 1933 WA which featured, along with others, engine enclosure to reduce the noise level and save the cost of polishing the hidden parts

Worthy, if unexciting model 3/1 for 1935, 343cc, side valves, limited performance, but well made in the house style.

Period advertisement for the Page twin of 1934, the 647cc model 6/1 which had its sidecar styled to match it.

One of the Val Page series of singles that came for 1934, this being the 493cc model 5/2, typical of the type and times.

Triumph offered this racing 493cc model 5/10 from 1934 to 1936, even entering a three-man team in the TT the first year, but all retired.

The sports 500 of 1936 was this model 5/5, much as the basic 5/2 and de luxe 5/4.

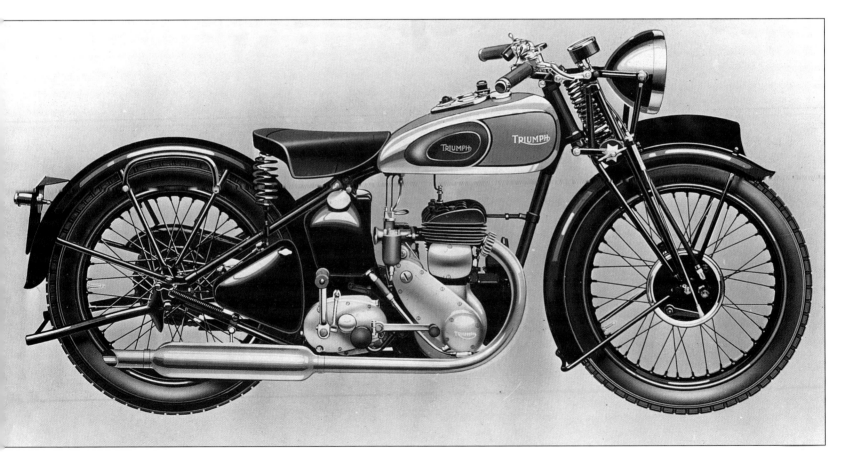

A brighter tank finish came for 1937, seen here on the 343cc model 3S de luxe.

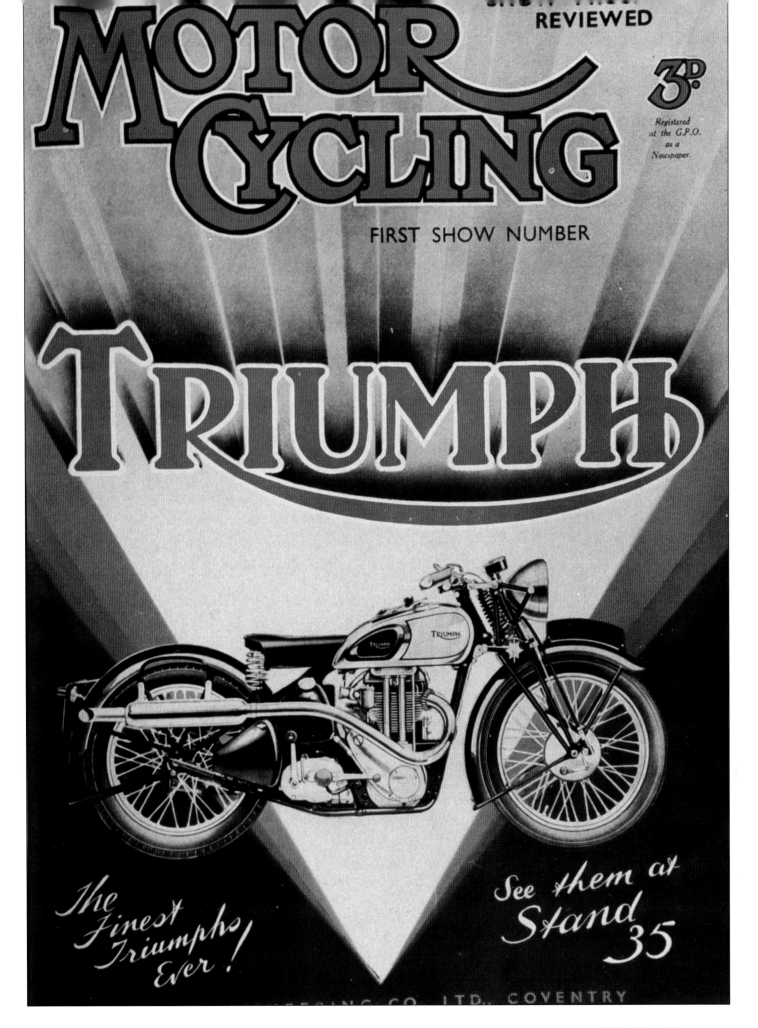

Advertisement for one of the three Tiger models introduced during 1936 to brighten up the Triumph range, a master stroke by Edward Turner.

TRIUMPH DE LUXE 6.S

84 m.m. by 108 m.m.
600 c.c. S.V.

PRICE: **£61**

Fully equipped with Lucas Magdyno
lighting and Electric Horn.

Valanced Guards, as illustrated, to order.
12 6 per pair extra.

A Smith illuminated Chronometric Trip Speedometer (80 m.p.h.)
will be supplied unless otherwise ordered, £2-10-0 extra.

New for the sidecar man in 1937 was this 599cc model 6S, built as the rest of the range but with more pulling power.

TURNER TWINS

L ate in 1937 came the Turner trend-setter, his 499cc Speed Twin which was to set the postwar trend and continued in outline form well into the 1980s. The brilliance of the Speed Twin lay in its compact design, small enough to use the cycle parts of the singles and actually lighter, a good performer and having a smooth, even, exhaust note. It was new and different, finished in a stylish amaranth red, but looked little altered from a twin-port single. It was an instant success.

Inevitably, it was joined by a Tiger 100 sports version for 1939, this having megaphone-style silencers and a black and silver sheen finish. Both twins were used for another attempt on the Maudes Trophy and late in the year, too late for interest, the firm learnt that they had again won it. For 1940 there should have been a 350 twin, built in touring and sports forms, to match the existing models. The outbreak of war brought these plans to an abrupt halt, the stock at Coventry being immediately requisitioned by the authorities.

First of the trend-setters, the prototype twin of 1937 seen outside the National Motorcycle Museum. The start of the legend.

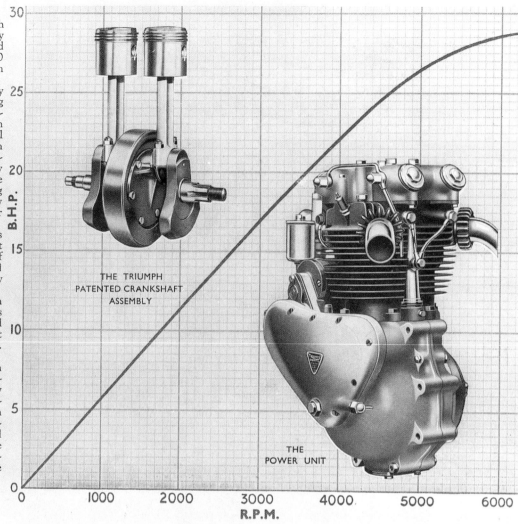

DESIGNED to combine a very high performance with the reliability which has always been associated with the name of Triumph the new 500 c.c. Speed Twin is a notable contribution to motor cycle development.

The cylinders are mounted vertically side by side, the crank assembly being such that even firing intervals are obtained. This form of construction results in an engine of extremely compact overall dimensions, and the whole layout with its massive crankcase and monobloc cylinder and head castings is particularly rigid and free from distortion. Ample air spaces are provided and the cooling arrangements are superior in every way to those obtainable with a single cylinder type of power unit.

Other advantages resulting from this compact layout are that excellent weight distribution is obtained and as a result of the modest overall height, both ground clearance and accessibility are highly satisfactory.

The use of hemispherical combustion chambers with short direct inlet ports is a feature of note, as is the special patented built-up construction of the crankshaft and the H-section connecting rods of R.R. 56 alloy with split type big-ends.

A high pressure dry-sump lubrication system making use of a pair of large capacity plunger pumps forces oil not only to all main bearings but also to the overhead valve gear, which attains a high standard of mechanical silence in operation. The bearing surfaces and general proportions throughout are such that the performance is maintained for long periods and the maintenance costs are therefore small.

THE TRIUMPH
PATENTED CRANKSHAFT
ASSEMBLY

THE
POWER UNIT

16

Above: Taken from the 1938 brochure, this shows the engine, crankshaft and power curve of the first Speed Twin.

63 mm. by 80 mm.
500 c.c. O.H.V.

PRICE: **£75**

Fully equipped with Lucas Magdyno lighting and Electric Horn.

A Smith illuminated Chronometric Trip Speedometer (120 m.p.h.) will be supplied unless otherwise ordered, £2-15-0 extra.

Timing side of the Speed Twin in its first year, also from the 1938 brochure.

Drive side of the 1939 Speed Twin showing a line that was to continue for many successful years.

The singles continued alongside the new twin, this being the 1938 Tiger 90 in its final year.

For 1939 Triumph introduced the Tiger 100 in place of the sports single and began another fine line. Note the megaphone silencers with their detachable ends.

TRIUMPH DE LUXE 3.H

70 m.m. by 89 m.m.
350 c.c. O.H.V.

PRICE: £56

*Fully equipped with Lucas Magdyno
lighting and Electric Horn.*

A Smith illuminated Chronometric Trip Speedometer (80 m.p.h.)
will be supplied unless otherwise ordered, £2-10-0 extra.

The 343cc model 3H as in 1938; it had some minor changes to become the wartime 3HW built in large numbers for service use.

WAR YEARS

The firm was then set to work to build singles for the services. Meanwhile, they used the 350 twin as the basis of a machine to meet a Ministry specification for a standard service model. If selected, it would be built by all suppliers, a lucrative commercial plum, and the twin was so well advanced that prototypes were quickly on test and as quickly approved as the chosen machine. Success lay in Triumph's hand until a fateful night in November 1940. Then came the blitz on Coventry and in the dawn the workforce found their factory in ruins. Fast action saw production underway in Warwick while a new factory was built on a site at Meriden, said to be the centre of England.

Meriden opened in 1942, while from 1941 the firm built 350 singles, most the ohv 3HW with a few side-valve machines thrown in. Work did continue on a military twin which led to the postwar TRW model sold mainly overseas into the 1960s. A wartime offshoot to have postwar effects was a generator unit built for the RAF. Based on the Speed Twin engine, it was fitted with a light-alloy top half of distinctive appearance.

The 350 twin built as the 3TW to suit a service specification but not to go into production. Based on a prewar design and to become a postwar model.

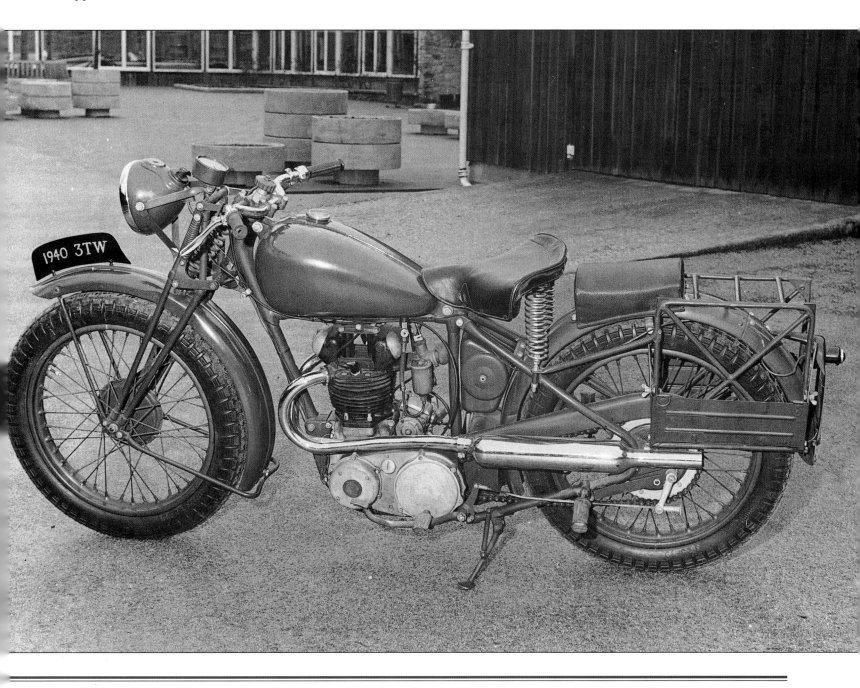

POST WAR YEARS

In March 1945 Triumph announced a five-model range of four twins and a single. In the event the single was never built as Triumph capitalised on their ten-year lead in the twin market and only three models reached production, the Speed Twin and Tiger 100 from prewar days, but fitted with telescopic front forks, and the 349cc 3T, a smaller and lighter tourer. During the late 1940s the Government screamed for production and exports so there were few changes, the most important the sprung rear hub which came in 1947.

The first effect of the wartime generator came in those years, its alloy top half a boon for competition, the outcome being a famous victory for Irishman Ernie Lyons in the 1946 Manx GP, and some Continental successes for David Whitworth in 1947. This led to the GP model in 1948, an out and out road racing machine based on the Tiger 100, but using race cams and the alloy top half. The result was competitive, fast but fragile.

The stillborn Tiger 85 sports twin of 1945 which did not go into production.

The 1945 349cc model 3T on which the T85 was based was built up to 1951 with little change.

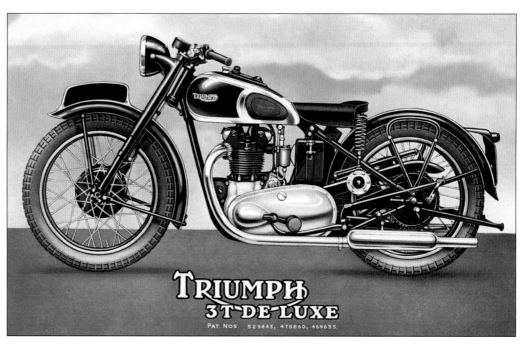

The postwar Tiger 100 had added telescopic front forks but was otherwise much as prewar.

Advertised as 'The twin with the 10-year lead', the postwar Speed Twin remained in the amaranth red used for many years.

Above: The Victory Parade held on June 8th, 1946, with the London police on their Speed Twins, a common sight in the city for many years.

Left: The early postwar Triumph tank and headlamp which were clean and tidy even before further efforts in that direction.

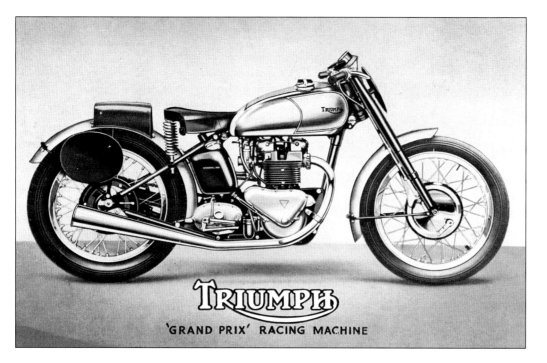

TRIUMPH

'GRAND PRIX' RACING MACHINE

The 499cc Grand Prix racing model built from 1948 to 1950, its alloy engine used wartime generator castings to good effect.

Below: Sectioned 1948 police Speed Twin on show in later years. Such exhibits involved a great deal of work to show the internals.

New for 1949 was the off-road TR5 model which used the alloy engine castings and had this stylish exhaust system. This one as seen in 1993

NACELLE, TERRIER & CUBS

For 1949 the headlamp nacelle was added to tidy the lines up. Its introduction cleared away the tank-top instrument panel which was replaced by a parcel grid, soon a firm favourite. The same year added the 499cc Trophy model, or TR5, for the off-road rider. Based on works machines ridden in the 1948 International Six Days Trial, it used the Speed Twin bottom half, alloy top half, a shorter frame and sports mudguards. Set off by a siamezed exhaust system and waist-level silencer, it had style and performed well both on and off the road.

A new and larger model was added for 1950, the 649cc Thunderbird, or 6T. Introduced by running a trio of machines round the Montlhéry bowl, near Paris, where all three covered 500 miles at a running average over 90 mph, it was much as the Speed Twin. Both models had a new tank style of four horizontal bars, the same theme decorating the Triumph stand at the Earls Court show that year.

A race kit appeared for the Tiger 100 in 1951, a year when that model adopted an alloy top half, also used by the TR5, and at the end of which the 3T was dropped. The race kit lasted for three years and for 1953 only the Tiger 100 was offered in T100c form which included the kit while the machine retained its full road equipment

Of more lasting effect was a new single introduced in 1953, destined to lead to many varieties and even a whole range for BSA! The machine was the 149cc Terrier, or T15, which had a simple overhead-valve engine, unit construction of its four-speed gearbox and the same style and line as the twins, down to the headlamp nacelle. During the next year it was joined by the 199cc Cub.

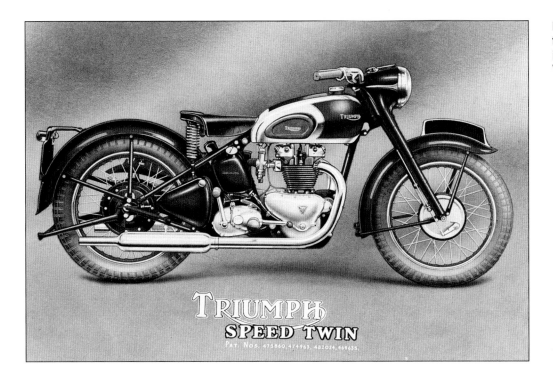

Left: For 1949 the tanktop panel gave way to the nacelle which combined the instruments in with the headlamp. Very tidy.

Below: The nacelle lacked an oil gauge but greatly improved the style of the machine, the feature remaining in use to 1966.

TRIUMPH

The Best Motorcycle in the World

The 1949 Triumph marks a new step forward in motorcycle design and development. The "Nacelle" design streamlines into the best possible position all the essential instruments, and presents a smooth and striking appearance. Along with many other improvements, its advent will be welcomed by practical hard riding motorcyclists as a further proof of Triumph determination to build the finest motorcycle possible today.

Triumph Engineering Co. Ltd., Meriden Works, Allesley, Coventry

Drive side of the 1949 Tiger 100, the one year that the old tank style was used with the new nacelle.

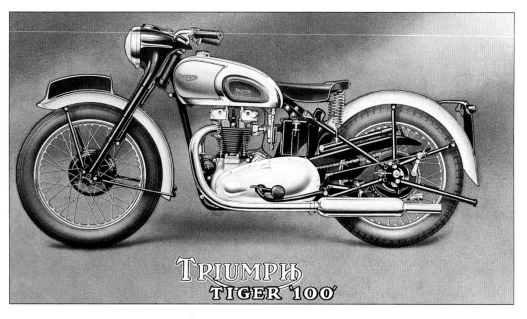

TRIUMPH
TIGER '100'

The 649cc Thunderbird model joined the range for 1950 when the four-bar tank decoration appeared. Faster than the Speed Twin and in its own colours.

The Best Motor Cycle in the World

TRIUMPH

From the wartime work came the side-valve TRW model for service use. Here the renowned Royal Signals display team collect their new machines from the Triumph works at Meriden.

The T15 Terrier of 149cc, introduced in 1953 as a Triumph in miniature with nacelle and tank badges.

The Thunderbird in its 1953 form and colour.

By 1953 the Speed Twin had alternator electrics but kept its traditional red finish.

TWO MAGNIFICENT SPORTING

The

TIGER 100 c

For 1953 only Triumph offered the T100c with twin carburettors, as well as a racing kit.

TRIUMPH
TIGER 100
500 c.c.

The sports Tiger 100 was still a highly rated machine in 1953, being fast and stylish.

NEW FRAMES

A sports version of the Thunderbird came in 1954 as the Tiger 110, having a pivoted-fork frame, bigger front brake and shell-blue finish, all features shared by the Tiger 100. For 1955 the other twins used that frame, including the TR5 which was tuned but lost some of its charm in the process. A 649cc version, the TR6, joined the range for 1956, its light-alloy cylinder head being used by the Tiger 110.

That year saw the end of the Terrier but this was followed by an expansion of the Cub range into off-road, competition and sports versions. All varieties were to continue to the mid-1960s, the Cub itself to 1969, albeit using many BSA Bantam cycle parts at the end.

Meanwhile, the twins ran on for the second half of the 1950s, enlivened by a 1956 bid by Johnny Allen on the world motorcycle record. Allen used a 649cc Triumph engine in his streamlined shell, ran at 214. 5 mph to set a new record, only to have his claim rejected on spurious grounds relating to the timing gear. Triumph took legal action, but without success.

Introduced for 1954, the Tiger 110 used the 649cc engine in a new pivoted-fork frame shared with the T100.

For 1954 the TR5 Trophy model continued little altered, being popular for going to work and weekend trials.

The 1955 Speed Twin went over to the pivoted-fork frame to give it a new style.

The frame also went onto the Thunderbird which copied the smaller twin in most respects.

Below: The Terrier which introduced the single range but was dropped after 1956.

The T20 Tiger Cub joined the Terrier during 1954 and went on to appear in many guises.

For 1956 the TR6 was added to the range, along with an alloy head for itself and the T110, but this is the companion TR5.

The record breaker ridden on Bonneville salt flats to over 214 mph by Johnny Allen late in 1956.

For 1957 the Tiger 110 was offered in these optional two-tone colours.

The 1957 Tiger 100 in its standard finish, still a most attractive machine.

Below: By 1957 the Tiger Cub had adopted a pivoted-fork frame and smaller wheels to create a most popular machine.

Both the TR5 and TR6 continued, but with changes which made them faster but less easy to ride off-road.

Amaranth red remained the finish for the Speed Twin which was dropped in this form after 1958 and two decades.

Below: Now relegated to a touring role, the 1957 Thunderbird in a new colour and black frame.

UNIT CONSTRUCTION

That 1957 year saw the first of a new unit-construction line, the 349cc model Twenty-One, so called to celebrate the 2lst birthday of Triumph Engineering and that the engine fell in the 21-cubic-inch class in the USA. At home it was simply the 3TA, a typical Meriden-built, ohv twin, having a four-speed gearbox and Triumph lines. What set it apart was its rear enclosure which managed an elegant line combined with good weather protection, not easy to achieve. Its shape soon earned it the name of 'bathtub'.

In 1959 the 3TA was joined by a 490cc version in amaranth red, listed as the 5TA, which replaced the old Speed Twin while keeping its name and colour. The same year saw the firm launch a new scooter range, also badged as a BSA, offering a 172cc two-stroke engine or a 249cc, ohv twin. Both had limited success, having arrived late in the day, and lacking the light touch of the leading Italian designs.

During 1957 Triumph introduced a unit-construction twin, the 349cc Twenty-One or 3TA, which heralded a new line to take over from the old.

Below: One of the many sports versions of the Tiger Cub, this being a T20S/S from 1962, but much as the earlier and later forms.

Above: London Airport police on their Speed Twins in front of a BEA VIscount.

The Hailwoods, père et fils, receiving a picture of Mike on his race-winning Tiger 110 from Edward Turner at Earls Court.

Above: Final form of the off-road TR6, still with the sexy exhaust system.

For 1959 a new form of the Speed Twin, the 5TA, was launched, based on the 3TA unit-construction twin. Here shown with the original model.

Above: Police Triumphs escort premier Harold Macmillan and his guest president Ike Eisenhower in central London,

Right: The Tigress scooter came in 1959 with the choice of 172cc two-stroke single – or 249cc four-stroke twin-cylinder engines.

BIRTH OF THE BONNEVILLE

The real Triumph event for 1959 was neither the 5TA nor the scooters, but a new sports 650 destined to become one of the great models of all time - the Bonneville. For some years the firm had listed twin-carburettor options for the Tiger models which were starting to be used in production racing. The Bonneville, listed as the T120, was the outcome of this trend and was essentially the T110 with a tuned engine, the twin-carburettor option, but no air filters. The name commemorated the world record run and the model was an immediate and long-lasting success. Its trend was to lead away from the enclosure theme to out-and-out sports machines - the café racer.

The start of the 1960s saw a replacement for the Tiger 100 in the form of the bland T100A, a sports version of the 5TA which retained the bathtub. Fortunately, it was soon replaced by the sparkling T100SS, a model fitted with an abbreviated rear enclosure, or skirt, and finished in bright colours. The 6T and T110 both gained the bathtub for 1960 but the Tiger 110 was dropped after 1961. That year saw the old TR6 gone but it then returned as a road model, effectively a single-carburettor version of the Bonneville.

Twin carburettors were fitted to the T110 Tiger to create the famous T120 Bonneville for 1959.

A 1962 Bonneville T120, the last year for the pre-unit type which established this highly esteemed model.

The unit-construction Speed Twin 5TA model first seen in 1959.

Both this **1961 Tiger 110**, in its final year, and the unit-construction T100A were built in this style with the bathtub.

The drab T100A soon gave way to this bright T100S/S of 1962 which led on to a popular series.

This 1962 road TR6S/S replaced the earlier model, essentially becoming a single carburettor Bonneville.

Thunderbird **650** c.c. / **6T**

The Thunderbird fitted the bathtub from 1960 to this 1962 machine which featured siamesed exhaust pipes.

By 1959 the Tiger Cub had been fitted with the skirt rear enclosure, this 1963 model also having the points moved into the timing cover.

Final year for the pre-unit Bonneville was 1962 when the finish was as bright as ever.

T he Tina, a 100cc scooter having automatic transmission, appeared for 1962, but it was 1963 that saw the next major revision when unit construction was adopted for the 649cc models - the Thunderbird, now with rear skirt, the TR6 Trophy, and the ever successful T120 Bonneville. That year, a sports version of the 3TA was added as the Tiger 90, mirroring the T100SS, and the Triumph range was set to run right through the 1960s.

Along the way the Tina became the T10, the larger scooters were dropped around 1965, the Cub continued in many forms, bathtubs and skirts went, and there were special versions of most twins for the American market. The touring models were dropped after 1966, a year when the marque won at Daytona, this resulting in a twin-carburettor Tiger 100 model carrying that circuit name.

A 100cc automatic scooter, the Tina, was launched in 1962 and later became this T10, neither making much impact on the market.

The Thunderbird adopted both unit construction and a skirt for 1963.

First unit-construction Bonneville was in 1963, after which the engine and gearbox were to change in detail only.

A single-carburettor twin continued as the 649cc TR6 Trophy model.

A sports 350 was introduced for 1963 as the Tiger 90, similar to the T100S/S and reviving a prewar name.

Triumph continued to do much police business with machines such as this, well able to stay with most vehicles on the road.

Sports Cub T20S/H as in 1964 when it was also listed in trials and scrambles forms.

By 1964 the Tiger 100 had lost its skirt as fashion turned away from enclosure, the Tiger 90 following suit.

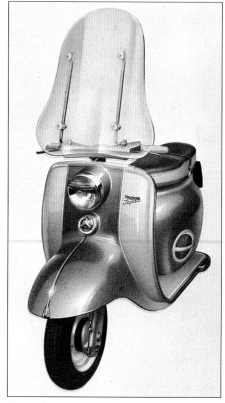

Above: The larger scooters came to an untidy end in 1965, never having sold too well in their market place.

Models for the USA:
Top right: Bonneville Speedmaster T120R whose high bars make the change.
Bottom right: Highway Trophy TR6SR with the single carburettor.

USA Bonneville "TT" Special T120C for off-road experts able to handle the weight and power from its open pipes.

USA Trophy Special TR6SC, also off-road but a single carburettor to make it better for all-day riding.

Back in the UK, Triumph built a small number of Thruxton Bonneville models for production racing. Very special with all the quick parts and most successful.

Bonneville T120 in its 1966 form, THE sports twin of the decade.

The TR6 was nearly as fast, often preferred by riders who used their machines every day of the week.

1966 was the final year for the Twenty-One and Speed Twin models which kept the nacelle although they lost their skirts in the end. This is the smaller twin.

The Tiger Cub had a new format for 1966, using many BSA Bantam parts and new colours, but losing both skirt and nacelle.

The Tiger 100 in its 1966 Sherbourne green and white, as popular as ever.

The off-road TR6C in its US West Coast form for 1966 when both pipes went on the left.

Bonneville T120/R as in its 1967 US road guise.

For the USA the Bonneville TT Special retained its twin open pipes tucked under the engine and gearbox.

The T20/M Mountain Cub was built for the US market and based on the sports and competition models sold at home.

New for 1967 was the T100T Daytona model fitted with a twin-carburettor version of the 490cc engine.

DECADE END AND TRIDENT

As the decade moved towards its end the Cub range shrunk and the off-road versions were replaced by the 247cc TR25W Trophy model, in reality a badge-engineered BSA model. Of far more importance was the appearance of the 740cc, three-cylinder Trident which was launched alongside a similar BSA model having an inclined engine. The Triumph, listed as the T150, kept its cylinders upright and used a style that could be seen to run back through the twins. It was an impressive motorcycle that was to perform well on the road and build an excellent racing record.

The 1960s were a period of great success for Triumph, sales being high both at home and abroad, especially in the USA. They had many successes in road racing at all levels, including wins at Daytona and in the Isle of Man. The Bonneville remained THE sports twin of the decade, and the Trident was set to continue the theme.

Final form of the small single was as the Super Cub whlch used more Bantam cycle parts but kept the falthful 199cc engine.

Super Value from the very centre of England—

..... the new TRIUMPH SUPER CUB 200

Here's a sparkling new addition to the Triumph range—the Super Cub 200—an attractive new version of the popular Tiger Cub.

It's nippy, easy to handle, economical to run, and in its new Flamboyant Bushfire Red, even more appealing in appearance than its predecessor.

Modern style petrol tank, chromium-plated headlamp, full-width hubs, new type dual seat with safety strap—these are new features which make the Super Cub super value.

Three cylinders made for the performance of the T150 Trident which began with the 'ray-gun' silencers seen on this 1970 example

The off-road 247cc Trophy TR25W model, a clone of a BSA which in turn was first based on the Terrier and Cub engines.

Bonneville T120 in its 1969 form with twin-leading-shoe front brake and twin windtone horns to announce its passage.

The 1970 Bonneville fitted with the smaller tank and high bars for the US market.

The Trident enjoyed a successful racing year in 1971, one being seen here refuelling at Daytona.

Daytona 500, twin-carburettor model for the USA as in 1970.

The Trophy 500 version of the smaller twin was intended for off-road, trail use, hence the raised pipes.

JOINT LAUNCH

The problem was the emergence of the larger Japanese models, and to combat this opposition Triumph and BSA joined forces and set up a common research laboratory at Umberslade Hall. The two firms had been linked commercially for some time and decided on a major revamp for 1971. This involved new machines, some common to both marques, and the use of common parts for many models. All were launched at a lavish preview for the trade and press.

It was one thing to lay on the launch party, quite another to deal with the many engineering and production problems that the new range and many major changes produced. Umberslade Hall had come up with a new frame for the 650s that carried the engine oil within its main tube. With it went new forks and wheel hubs plus a host of new detail parts, but the crux of the problem was an excessive seat height. Before production could start this had to be remedied which in turn meant many detail changes.

Meanwhile the Tiger 100 models, fortunately little altered, could be built, but a 349cc ohc twin was simply dropped at considerable cost, as were other projects. The 247cc single was revised to a new, oil-bearing frame, group forks, group hubs and many other changes, to be offered in street-scrambler or trail formats, still mimicking the BSA models they were based on.

In time the reduced range reached production but the whole group was by then in serious financial difficulties from which BSA were not to survive. Triumph and its future became a political matter which climaxed late in 1973 with the famous sit-in by the Meriden workforce that was to last for 18 months.

During the run-up to this traumatic time, the range began to move to its final form. The two singles went at the end of 1971, but a 499cc moto-cross model was built for 1973-74 It was listed as the TR5MX Avenger, had an odd exhaust system using one pipe but two silencers in parallel, and was really a BSA B50MX with

Triumph badges.

The Tiger 100 twins were little changed, the road model running on to 1974, the off-road to 1972 when it was replaced by the TR5T which used the singles frame and was listed as the Trophy Trail or Adventurer. It too ran to 1974.

The Trident continued for 1971 with new forks and hubs, went over to a five-speed gearbox during 1972 and was joined by the X75 Hurricane in 1973. This last was built in a custom style designed by Craig Vetter and used the BSA inclined engine, the BSA frame and extended forks. Its prime features were to have all three exhausts on the right, and a combined tank cover plus seat base in red. It was only built for the one year, during which the Trident was fitted with a disc front brake.

Meanwhile, the 650s struggled into production as the T120R Bonneville, the TR6R Tiger 650 for the road, and the TR6C Trophy 650 with waist level exhaust systems for trail use. Five-speed gearboxes appeared for 1972 and the disc front brake for 1973 when the first of the 744cc models joined the range as the T140 Bonneville and TR7 Tiger. These continued the theme of single and twin-carburettor versions of the same machine but fitted with the five-speed gearbox and disc front brake from the start.

Trident for 1971 with conical hubs and new front brake that was less than effective for its speed and weight.

Below: For 1971, the Daytona 500 remained much as before so missed the trauma of the group changes.

One of the two stillborn 350cc overhead-camshaft twins was this Bandit SS 350 aimed at the trail-machine market.

The Bandit 350 road model was the other dropped twin, both of which used the group forks and wheels, both models being duplicated as BSAs.

As with the 350, the 247cc single was listed in road and trail form and as a BSA, This is the Blazer SS 250 version.

Below: For 1973 the 490cc trail model became this TR5T, known as the Adventurer or the Trophy Trail, but it lacked the line of the original TR5.

The Trident in its 1972 form for the home market which kept the large fuel tank,

Hurricane X75 of 1973 which used the BSA version of the triple engine and had its own special style.

A 1971 Bonneville T120R out on road test in the British countryside.

As part of the new image, the TR6 became the TR6R Tiger 650 for the road and the TR6C Trophy 650 for the trail.

Front disc brake finally came for the Bonneville in 1973 along with five speeds to create the T120V.

For 1973 Triumph enlarged the twins to 744cc to produce the T140 Bonneville and this TR7RV Tiger.

STRIKE – AND CO-OP

Then came the Meriden sit-in and turmoil. It ran until March 1975 before a workers' co-operative was set up, although this was by no means the end of the firm's problems. The effect was that production of the smaller twins ceased, the Trident line was moved to the BSA works at Small Heath, while the larger twins remained at Meriden.

The Trident was revised for 1975 to become the T160, using the BSA inclined engine, but fitted with Triumph-style timing covers. The Triumph frame was retained, and an electric starter, rear disc brake and left gearchange added. In this form it ran on for 1976 when its production ceased.

Of the 650 twins, the TR6 models stopped late in 1973, only the five-speed T120 continuing as a 1974 model, production ending early in 1975. From mid-1975 the factory built only the 750s, and these took a form to suit the USA, having a disc rear brake and left gearchange. From then to the end of 1982, Meriden struggled on, having some success, but always carrying debt and cash-flow problems. The staff tried very hard, introducing new versions of the basic machine to try to capture every possible sale.

End of the Trident line came with a batch of Cardinal police machines having a single seat.

US-style bars for a 1973 Trident which had the front disc brake and five-speed gearbox by then.

Final form of the Trident was as the T160, built for 1975 with the inclined engine and rear disc brake

Above: The 744cc TR7V of 1976, by when it had a left-side gear pedal and rear disc brake.

Left: The 1979 T140E Bonneville American which had high bars and a small tank.

For the T140E Bonneville European the tank and bars were changed, both versions being offered in alternative colours.

The single-carburettor TR7 was also offered in both US and European forms, various colours, and listed as the Tiger 750.

JUBILEE – BUT MERIDEN CLOSES

Thus, 1977 saw the Jubilee model to celebrate 25 years of Queen Elizabeth's reign, there was the T140D Special of 1979 having cast-alloy wheels, the Royal of 1981 when Prince Charles and Lady Di married, and the Executive fitted with fairing, screen, panniers and top box. The basic Bonneville simply ran on, still the favourite for many riders who appreciated its simplicity, good handling and sheer style.

As the 1980s came along Triumph built a prototype Low Rider, introduced a Trail model, tried a smaller economy version of 649cc, later went down to a couple of 599cc models, offered an lsolastic system to insulate the rider from vibration, and tried an eight-valve head on an alloy block. All were good efforts but none were able to halt the slow decline and in the end the money just ran out.

This stylish T140D Bonneville Special was added for 1979, having cast-alloy wheels and an all-black finish with gold lining.

Above: European version of the Bonneville Royal of 1981, a limited edition celebrating the Prince Charles and Lady Di marriage.

Left: During 1980 this Executive model was added, fitted as standard with fairing, panniers and top box.

Above: Another avenue was the 744cc Tiger Trail first seen at the Paris show as a 1981 model. A 649cc version was also built.

Another 1981 model was this 649cc Thunderbird which revived old-time memories and was built as a low-budget machine.

New for 1982 was this TSS model which had an all alloy, eight-valve engine and the option of an anti-vibration frame.

Left: Matching the TSS was this TSX, a custom version with alloy wheels, the rear a 16 inch, high bars and two-level seat.

RACING SPARES

Meriden production ceased at the start of 1983; the firm went into liquidation, was sold off, and finally the famous factory was demolished. It should have been the end - in fact it was the start of something new, for the name was bought by businessman John Bloor who licensed Racing Spares to produce the Bonneville for five years.

Racing Spares were already making Triumph parts, so were in a good position to produce complete machines. The deal was for them to build the Bonneville in its final form without major change which kept the name alive while Bloor put his plans into operation. These were nothing less than to create a new factory on a green-field site at Hinckley in which he intended to build a totally new range of Triumphs.

And so it happened. Racing Spares built Bonnevilles in Devon from 1985 to 1988 while Bloor set to work in total secrecy. The wraps were kept on so well that it was 1989 before any news emerged, and then only to indicate an engine having three or four cylinders, twin-overhead camshafts, four valves per cylinder and water cooling.

The US version of the Bonneville as built down in Devon by Racing Spares after Meriden closed.

HINCKLEY
· · · · · · · · · · · · · · · · ·

The new range was launched in September 1990 at the Cologne show, and comprised six models sharing a common concept and many detail parts. The inline engines had three or four cylinders and a long or short stroke, but all shared the same bore, four-valve combustion chamber, chain-driven twin-overhead camshafts and water cooling. The capacities of the triples were 748 or 885cc and that of the fours was 998 or 1179cc. Each cylinder was fed unleaded petrol by a 36mm Mikuni carburettor and this was fired by electronic ignition, the trigger for this fitted at one end of the crankshaft.

Inside the engine went one or two balancer shafts to reduce vibration, while the generator and starter were behind the block to reduce width. Gear primary drive to a six-speed gearbox built in unit was used, final drive was by chain, and the engine castings were given form and style to enable them to be a design feature.

The engine hung from a tubular spine frame and suspension was by Kayaba telescopic forks and a rising-rate rear unit. Triple-spoke, cast-alloy wheels fitted with Nissin disc brakes were used, their size and that of the tyres varying a little from model to model although all had twin front discs and a single rear. Thus, most of the cycle side was common.

1990 Prototype Daytona 750 triple.

Three pairs of models were listed, each pair offered with an engine choice. Basic were the Trident 750 and 900 triples which had no fairing and relied on the engine, tank and side panels for their style. Next came the Trophy 900 triple and 1200 four, sports-tourers having a fairing, and lastly the Daytona 750 triple and 1000 four sports models which had a fairing fitted with twin headlamps.

The range had a good reception which was followed by excellent road test reports. There was no doubt - this was serious business and Triumph had got it right. While production built up, little, other than colour, was changed for 1992.

For 1993 the two Daytonas were replaced by new versions and there were two new models. The replacement Daytonas were the 900 triple and 1200 four, the latter available with a 147bhp engine. New was the Trident Sprint 900, which had a half fairing and the twin headlamps, and the Tiger 900, a Super Moto/Enduro triple. For its occasional off-road use it had a detuned engine and various chassis changes to frame, wheels, tyres, suspension, seat and tank. It was fitted with the half fairing.

The whole range was improved for 1994 to go forward with two additions, both using the 885cc triple engine. First was the Speed Triple in a classic café racer format finished in black and yellow. Second came the Daytona Super III which had a tuned, but lighter, engine developing 115bhp, six-piston callipers for the front discs, carbon fibre parts and a full fairing. Aimed at the sports-machine market, its announcement came with plans to extend the factory.

Triumph continue to build good motorcycles.

1990 Prototype Daytona 1000 four.

1990 Prototype Trophy 900 triple.

Below: 1990 Prototype Trophy 1200 four.

1991 Trident 900 triple.

1992 Trident 750 triple.

1992 Daytona 1000 four.

1992 Trident 900 triple, very popular.

1991 Trophy 1200 four

1993 Daytona 1200 first seen late in 1992, fitted with 147 bhp engine.

Below: Trident 900 triple for 1992. This model was a good seller, the engine the most popular type.

Above: 1993 Tiger 900 enduro model
launched late in 1992.

Right: 1993 Daytona 1200..

1993 Daytona 900.

1993 Trophy 1200 four.

1993 Trophy 900 triple.

1993 Tiger 900 triple.

1993 Trident Sprint 900 triple.

The 1993 Trophy 1200 four, half the Triumph sales were of the Trophy models.

1994 Speed Triple

1994 Daytona Super III

TRIUMPH MODELS

SINGLES

4 hp	H, D, SD
100 t/s	Tina, T10
150 t/s	Z, XV/l
150 ohv	X0, X05, T15
175 t/s	X, TSl
175 ohv	X07
200 ohv	T20, T20C, T20S, T20T, T20S/L, T20S/S, T20S/H, T20SC, T20SR. TS20, TR20 T20SM, T20M, Bantam Cub, Super Cub
225/250 t/s	LW
250 ohv	WO, WA, WP, 2/1, 2/5, L2/1, T70, 2H, 2HC, TR25W, T25SS, T25T
278 sv	W, WS
350 sv	LS, WL, 3/1, 3S, 3SC, 3SE, 3SW
350 ohv	CO, NM, CA, 3/2, 3/5, T80, 3H, 3HW
500 sv	P, N, QA, NP, NL, CN, 5S, 5SE, 5SW
500 ohv	R, TT, ST, CTT, NT, CD, B, BS, 5/2, 5/4, 5/5, 5/10, T90, 5H, TR5MX
550 sv	H, D, SD, NSD, CSD, ND, A, 5/1, 5/3
600 sv	6S

TWINS

250 ohv	TW2, TW2S
350 ohv	3TW, 3T, 3TA, T90
500 sv	5TW, TRW
500 ohv	5T, T100, GP, TR5, 5TA, T100A, T100SS, T100S, T100T, T100R, T100C, TR5T
600 ohv	Thunderbird, Daytona 600
650 ohv	6/1, 6T, T110, TR6, T120, TR6R, TR6C, T120R, T120C, T120TT, T120 Thruxton, TR6RV, TR6CV, T120V, T120RV, T65, TR65, TR65T
750 ohv	TR7RV, TR7V, TR7T, T140V, T140RV, T140 Jubilee, T140D, T140E, T140ES, T140 Executive, T140 Royal, T140TSS, T140TSX, Devon T140

TRIPLES

750 ohv	T150, T150V, X75, T160

HINCKLEY TRIUMPHS

Trlples	Trident 750, Trident 900, Trident Sprint 900, Trophy 900, Daytona 750, Daytona 900, Tiger 900, Speed Triple, Daytona Super III
Fours	Trophy 1200, Daytona 1000, Daytona 1200

TRIUMPH MODEL NAMES

Adventurer TR5T	Thunderbird 6T
Avenger TR5MX	Tiger 90 T90
Blazer T25SS	Tiger 100 T100
Bonneville T120, T140	Tiger 110 T110
Cub T20	Tiger TR6, TR7
Daytona T100T, T100R	Trail Blazer T25T
Grand Prix GP	Trident T150, T160
Hurricane X75	Trophy TR5, TR6, TR7
Speed Twin 5T, 5TA	Trophy Trail TR5T
Terrier T15	Twenty One 3TA